MW01254389

Pearson Baccalaureate PYP Readers

Twiga and the Moon

Frances Usher
Illustrated by Stephen Lewis

In Africa there was a beautiful river.
By the river were tall trees
and lots of green grass.
Next to the river lived a little giraffe
called Twiga.

Day after day Twiga walked about
by the river with the other giraffes.
The big giraffes were tall so they
could eat the leaves from up in
the trees.

Twiga's father was the tallest of all
the giraffes and he could eat the
beautiful leaves at the very top
of the tall trees.

But Twiga could only
eat the leaves from
the little trees.
'I wish I was tall
like you,' said Twiga
to his father.
'One day you will be
as tall as I am,'
said his father.

That made Twiga very happy.
He said to the other giraffes,
'One day I will be as tall as my father
and I will eat the beautiful leaves
at the very top of the tall trees.'

Twiga said, 'Then one day I will be
the tallest giraffe in Africa.'
'Is that so?' said the other giraffes.
'And what will you eat then?'

Twiga looked up.

He saw the moon up in the sky.

'I will eat that,' he said.

'You can't eat the moon,' said
the other giraffes.

'Why not?' said Twiga. 'I think it
looks very good to eat.'

The other giraffes all laughed.

Twiga said no more about eating the
moon but he did not forget about it.
Night after
night he would
look up at
the moon and
think about
eating it up.
How cold
it would be
in his mouth.

One night it was very hot and Twiga
could not sleep. He looked up at
the sky but the moon had gone.
'Where is the moon?' he said.
'Where is my beautiful moon?'

Then all the other giraffes looked up.

'The moon has gone,' they said.

'Someone must have eaten it.'

The giraffes all laughed.

Then the rain came.

All the giraffes went under the trees
and it rained

and rained

and rained.

Twiga wished the rain would stop.
'Where has the moon gone?' he asked
his father. 'Has someone eaten it?'
'No,' said his father. 'The moon
will come back. You will see.'

The rain stopped. The giraffes came
out from the trees and walked about
by the river.
Twiga looked up at the sky.
'Look,' he said. 'The moon is back.
When I am tall can I eat the moon?'

'You can't eat the moon,' said Twiga's
father. 'But I will show you something
that you can eat when you grow up.'
He gave Twiga some beautiful fruit
from the top of a very tall tree.
'Mmmm, that's good,' said Twiga.

The next day the other giraffes
asked Twiga, 'What are you going
to eat today?'
'I'm going to eat the little leaves just here,'
said Twiga. 'Then I will grow tall and
eat the beautiful fruit at the top of
the trees, just like my father.'